Endangered and Threatened Animals

POLAR BEARS

by Kathy Allen

Consultant:
Andrew A. Derocher, PhD
Professor, Department of Biological Sciences
University of Alberta
Edmonton, Alberta, Canada

CAPSTONE PRESS
a capstone imprint

Snap Books are published by Capstone Press,
1710 Roe Crest Drive, North Mankato, Minnesota 56003.
www.capstonepub.com

Library of Congress Cataloging-in-Publication Data
Allen, Kathy.
 Polar bears / by Kathy Allen.
    p. cm. — (Snap books. Endangered and threatened animals.)
 Includes bibliographical references and index.
 Summary: "Describes the life cycle and characteristics of polar bears, including physical
and environmental threats to the species"—Provided by publisher.
 ISBN 978-1-4296-8432-3 (library binding)
 ISBN 978-1-62065-349-4 (ebook PDF)
 1. Polar bear—Juvenile literature. I. Title.

QL737.C27A52 2013
599.786—dc23   2011046681

Editor: Mari Bolte
Designer: Bobbie Nuytten
Media Researcher: Marcie Spence
Production Specialist: Kathy McColley

Photo Credits:
Alamy: louise murray, 23, Robert Harding Picture Library Ltd., 15; Corbis: Kennan Ward, 16, Wayne Lynch/
All Canada Photos, 29; PSmicrographs, 9 (top right); Shutterstock: Bernhard Richter, 9 (top middle), Boris
Mrdja, 21 (ice melting), Denis Dryashkin, 28, Dudarev Mikhail, 21 (power plant), elm, 25, FloridaStock,
6, Jan Martin Will, 7, Julien, 21 (sniper), Juris Sturainis, design element, kaczor58, 21 (house), Laurent
Renault 21 (globe), myVector, 9 (bottome left), pavelmayorov, cover, Sylvie Bouchard, 11, Thomas Barrat,
9 (top left), Uryadnikov Sergey, 13, 18, 22, Volodymyr Krasyuk, 27, Wild Arctic Pictures, design element, 9
(bottom right), 12, Yuliyan Velchev, 25, Yvonne Pijinenburg-Schonewille, 5

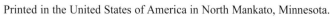

Printed in the United States of America in North Mankato, Minnesota.
042012   006682CGF12

Table of Contents

Chapter 1

Bear of the North

A blinding snowstorm rages at the top of the world. Long winters cover huge spans of ice and snow in darkness. The winter darkness in the Arctic lasts for months. The Arctic is one of the harshest places to live on Earth. But even in this punishing place life is rich. Ringed seals glide in the water between ice **floes**. A beluga whale swims under the ice, searching for prey.

But the whale is only interested in fish for dinner. The serious predator is the polar bear lurking nearby. The hunter crouches low in the snow, as white as its surroundings. Suddenly the tip of a seal's nose appears in a hole in the ice. Wide paws and sharp claws reach into the water. They pull the seal onto land. The polar bear has caught its next meal.

There are 19 recognized populations of polar bears in five different countries.

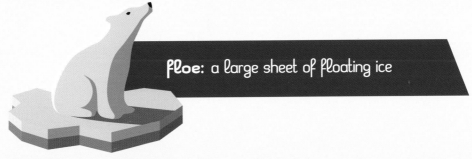

floe: a large sheet of floating ice

The amount a polar bear eats depends on how much it weighs. On average a polar bear eats between 10 and 20 percent of its body mass at every meal.

This great Northern bear is at the top of the Arctic food chain. Unlike other bears, polar bears eat **blubber**. They prefer the blubber of ringed seals and bearded seals. To go with their diet of blubber, bears eat anything that gives them energy. Some foods include fish, seabirds and their eggs, and even beluga whales and walruses!

In some cases, a bear will eat the blubber from an animal and discard the rest of the kill. The meat alone does not provide enough **calories** for the polar bear to survive.

Polar bears fear no natural enemies except other polar bears. But the largest of the living bears is still in danger.

Polar bears hunt on the sea ice. In winter, ice covers 90 percent of the ocean's surface. Bears walk across the ice to hunt. But during the summer, the ice melts. Polar bears need to swim from one ice patch to another to find food. But **climate change** is causing the ice to freeze later and melt earlier. As a result, the bears must live off the fat stored in their bodies for longer periods of time.

Bears have to swim greater distances too. The long swim at sea is hard on their bodies. If tired or weak, bears drown. Without help, the next 100 years may be the end of the great white bear.

A polar bear can swim as far as 62 miles (100 kilometers) between ice floes at a time.

blubber: fat used by some animals for energy, floating, and keeping warm

calorie: the amount of energy that food gives you

climate change: a significant change in Earth's climate

Chapter 2

The Great White Bear

One look at the polar bear reveals why it knows no fear. Male polar bears weigh between 900 and 1,600 pounds (408 and 726 kilograms). They are more than 8 feet (2.4 meters) long from their nose to their tail. Females are much smaller, about 300 to 500 pounds (136 to 227 kg). But at nearly 7 feet (2.1 meters) long, even the female is an impressive size.

Polar bears are well-adapted to life in the Arctic. A double layer of fur protects them from cold. Although their fur looks white, each hair is actually a clear hollow tube. The hollow hair helps the bear float while swimming. Blubber beneath their fur can reach layers as thick as 4 inches (10 centimeters). Blubber is another way the bear keeps warm. Even the soles of the polar bears' feet have fur to grip the ice. A polar bear's wide paws act like snowshoes to help it walk across ice.

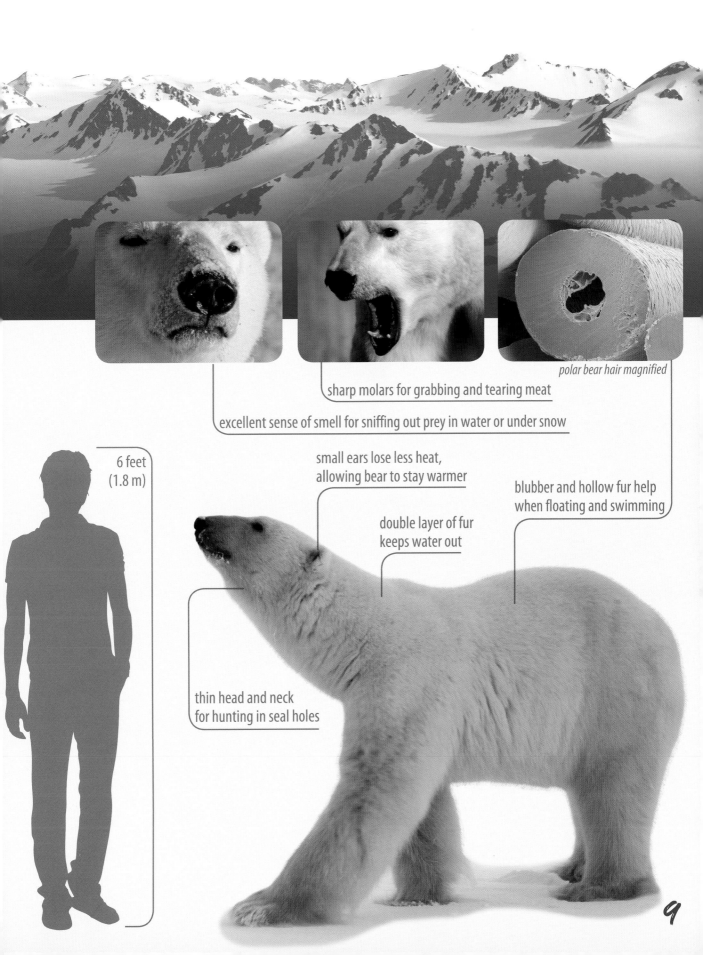

polar bear hair magnified

sharp molars for grabbing and tearing meat

excellent sense of smell for sniffing out prey in water or under snow

small ears lose less heat, allowing bear to stay warmer

blubber and hollow fur help when floating and swimming

double layer of fur keeps water out

6 feet (1.8 m)

thin head and neck for hunting in seal holes

9

Habitat and Range

The polar bear's amazing body allows it to live in one of the toughest places on Earth. The Arctic surrounds the North Pole. In winter, polar bears live where the sea freezes over along the coasts of Canada, Alaska, Russia, and Greenland. They drift on the sea ice and follow seals.

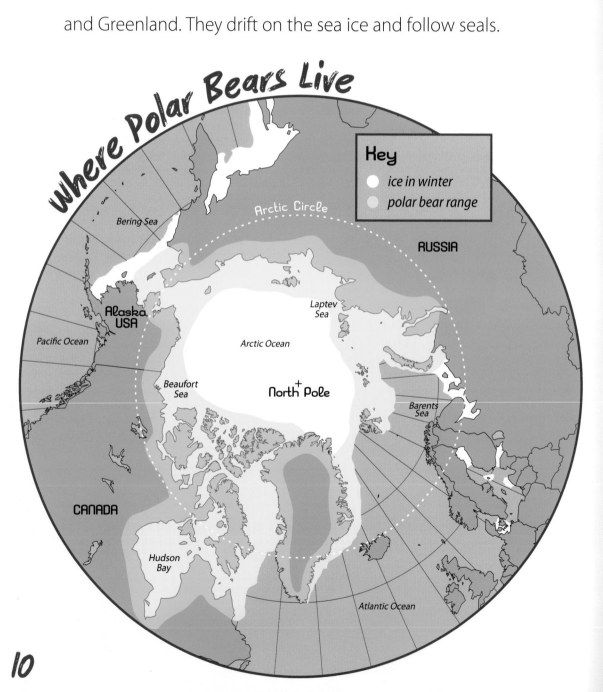

Where Polar Bears Live

Key
- ice in winter
- polar bear range

Arctic Circle

Bering Sea

RUSSIA

Laptev Sea

Alaska, USA

Arctic Ocean

Pacific Ocean

Beaufort Sea

North Pole

Barents Sea

CANADA

Hudson Bay

Atlantic Ocean

Polar bears prefer the ice near shorelines and over shallow water. Whale carcasses wash up on shore and seals come on land to give birth to pups early in the year. Both provide easy meals for bears. The currents in shallow water prevent the winter ice from getting too thick. But this ice begins to melt in the spring and summer. The ice melt starts in the southern part of the bear's range. Family groups and young bears usually move inland and closer to people. Others retreat northward to the ice that is too thick to melt.

Polar bears eat the most between April and July. During this time, pregnant bears need to build up their fat stores. But bears that spend summer on land don't have access to their usual food sources.

Land is a dangerous place to be for an animal that survives on the blubber of sea creatures. Whales or seals are rarely found on land. The bears must scavenge for any food they can find. Polar bears use twice as much energy than other mammals while walking or running. Scavenging quickly uses up the bear's fat stores.

The Hudson Bay area polar bears have seen big changes. Average body weights, skull sizes, and number of cubs born have dropped over the past 20 years.

Hunting

In the spring, polar bears spend most of the day hunting. They need a high-fat diet to survive. To build up their fat stores, polar bears follow their nose. Their amazing sense of smell helps find ringed and bearded seals on ice. Polar bears wait for hours near small holes in the ice. Seals use these holes to breathe. When a seal uses the hole to catch a breath of air, a polar bear is waiting.

Seals need to surface for air every five to 15 minutes. However, they will have a number of holes they use. A bear may wait hours or days for a seal to surface at one particular hole.

Polar bears stalk seals on ice by sneaking up on them. Their white coats help them blend in. When the bear is about 20 feet (6 meters) away, it rushes in. It catches its prey before the seal can escape into the sea.

Polar bears can run 18.5 miles (30 km) per hour to catch their next meal. They can even smell seal pups resting in snow dens. To catch these seals, they crash down on the seal's den. Then they grab their prey in a flurry of flying snow.

Polar bears also swim to hunt seabirds and ducks, although with less success. They use their front legs to paddle and their hind legs for steering. They hunt the birds by swimming underwater. They attack the birds from below. However, they are often unsuccessful. They are not fast swimmers and their prey often has time to escape.

The Life of a Polar Bear

Chapter 3

Female polar bears mate every two to three years between March and May. However, the embryo will not begin to develop for another four months. This slow start gives the female time to gain weight and store energy to raise her cubs. It also allows her to find a quiet place for a den.

Pregnant polar bears build dens to prepare for their new families. They build their dens in snowbanks. Some dens are built close to shore. Others have been seen more than 50 miles (80 km) from the ocean.

Females raise cubs without help from the male. Raising cubs is hard work. Some bears do not produce cubs if they are not able to gather enough energy. Others have been known to abandon their dens if they are too close to humans.

Polar bear cubs are called "coys" during their first year of life. This stands for "cubs of the year."

Sometimes a polar bear will rest in a den during bad weather. But pregnant bears spend months in their dens **hibernating**. Polar bears hibernate differently than other animals. They do not enter a deep sleep. But their bodies reach a lower temperature, and their heart and breathing rates slow.

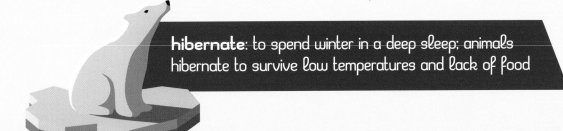

hibernate: to spend winter in a deep sleep; animals hibernate to survive low temperatures and lack of food

Polar bear cubs are born during some of the darkest, coldest winters on Earth. After the embryo begins to develop, cubs are born about 60 days later. Female bears usually give birth to two cubs, but sometimes one or three are born. Newborns weigh about 2 pounds (0.9 kg) at birth. A thin coat of fur covers their body. They are born blind. What will one day be a ferocious roar is now no louder than a tiny cry.

Polar bears and their cubs stay in the den all winter. The cubs grow strong on their mother's fat-rich milk. When spring arrives, the cubs venture out of the den for the first time. They are much larger now, weighing around 22 pounds (10 kg). They tussle and play with their mother and follow her every move.

By this time, the mother bear will have been without food for as long as eight months. She has used up most of her fat stores and is ready to hunt. She leads her cubs to the sea ice to teach them to hunt. Growing cubs are hungry and will nurse for the first 2½ years of their lives. After that, they must live on their own.

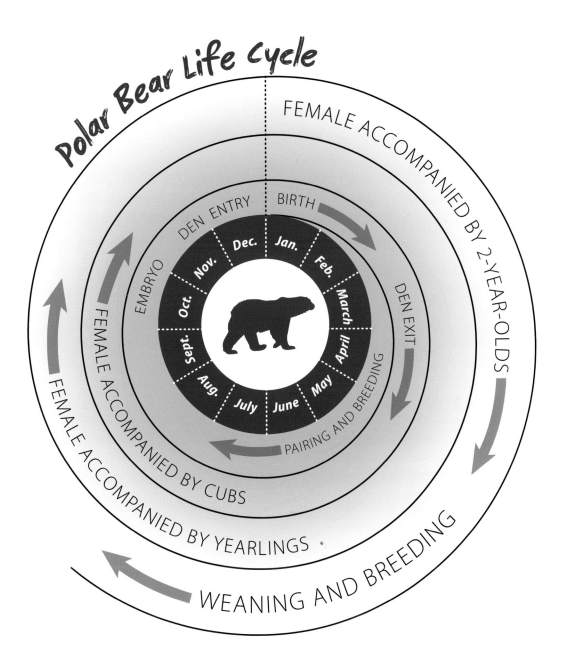

Polar Bear Life Cycle

FEMALE ACCOMPANIED BY 2-YEAR-OLDS

DEN ENTRY

BIRTH

EMBRYO

DEN EXIT

Dec.
Nov.
Oct.
Sept.
Aug.
July
June
May
April
March
Feb.
Jan.

FEMALE ACCOMPANIED BY CUBS

PAIRING AND BREEDING

FEMALE ACCOMPANIED BY YEARLINGS

WEANING AND BREEDING

A tired mother might not be able to make enough milk to feed her cubs. She also could be too weak to fight off predators, such as wolves or adult male bears. Adult bears may attack cubs for many reasons. They may be trying to control the bear population or to show dominance. Very hungry or starving bears may kill cubs for food.

A cub's chances of survival depend on the amount of available food—both for themselves and their mother. Hungry bears of any age have a hard time staying alive. Poor ice conditions mean poor hunting, which means not enough to eat. Cubs with inexperienced mothers have a high death rate too. Not knowing how to find enough food can be a death sentence for cubs.

If a polar bear cub reaches adulthood, it becomes a top predator. Adult polar bears live between 20 and 30 years in the wild. Today there are 20,000 to 25,000 wild polar bears. But there are populations of polar bears that are declining. What could threaten an animal that has no predators?

Polar bear cubs grow quickly on their mothers' milk, which is around 30 percent fat.

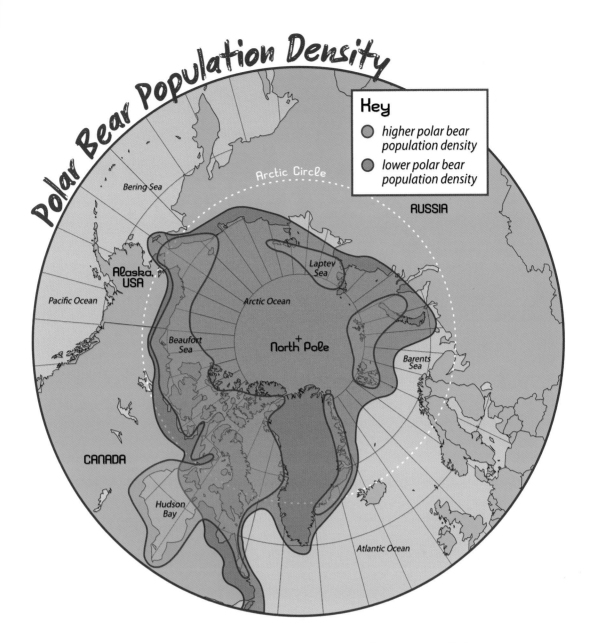

Polar Bear Population Density

Key
- higher polar bear population density
- lower polar bear population density

Arctic Circle

RUSSIA

Bering Sea

Laptev Sea

Alaska, USA

Pacific Ocean

Arctic Ocean

Beaufort Sea

North Pole

Barents Sea

CANADA

Hudson Bay

Atlantic Ocean

Today the bears' hunting period is shorter and there is less ice to hunt on. Over the past 25 years, the sea ice has decreased from 4.8 million square miles (12.4 million square kilometers) to 4.4 million square miles (11.4 million square km). Bears are not growing as large and have less fat. Female bears are giving birth to fewer cubs. And the cubs are having a harder time reaching adulthood.

A Threatened Species

Polar bears face a number of threats, including global warming. The Arctic is warmer than it has been in the past 400 years. The warmer temperatures melt the sea ice that polar bears need to hunt. It also takes away the habitat seals need to survive. With the melting ice, the bears must swim farther between ice floes to find enough to eat. Sometimes they can't make the long distances.

In 2008 scientists followed a cub with its mother that tried to swim more than 425 miles (684 km) to the ice. The cub never reached its final destination.

What Are Greenhouse Gases?

Global warming is caused by **greenhouse gases**. These are gases from:

- burning fuel from cars and other vehicles
- using electricity
- factories
- landfills
- burning coal
- grazing animals such as cows

greenhouse gas: gases in a planet's atmosphere that trap heat energy from the sun

Threats to the Polar Bear

GLOBAL WARMING

HABITAT LOSS

HUMAN DEVELOPMENT

POLLUTION

HUNTING

Contact with humans is not safe for any wild animal, including polar bears. But the polar bears' quest for food has forced the two species together. Recently hungry polar bears have been spotted hundreds of miles inland. They smell food in houses and come looking for something to eat. Some bears spend the summer eating the garbage people throw away. In one area, dozens of bears gather during an Inuit tribe's annual whale hunt.

Attacks on humans are rare, but contact between bears and humans is increasing. Hungry bears are attracted to the trash humans leave behind. Bears may enter towns or villages looking for an easy meal. Many polar bears are shot every year by people defending their homes.

Hunting is also a threat. In the 1960s and 1970s, being hunted by humans was the greatest threat to polar bears. In 1973 a meeting was held. The countries where polar bears lived—Canada, Denmark (for Greenland), the United States, Norway, and the former USSR (now Russia)—signed an agreement. They agreed to limit the hunting of polar bears. However, the bears are still being hunted. Today more than 600 polar bears are hunted around the world each year, and interest continues to grow.

Polar Bears and the Inuit

For centuries, native people called the Inuit hunted the polar bear for clothing and food. The bear's hide was hung inside their homes. Offerings were made to the powerful animal they called Nanook, or the Great White Bear.

The Inuit still hunt polar bears today, both by themselves and as guides. Canada is the only country that allows outsiders to trophy hunt polar bears. Sport hunters, usually Americans, bring more than $1.5 million to the Inuit communities annually. A 2011 ban prevents American hunters from bringing any part of the bear across the border. Still, about 300 Canadian polar bears are hunted each year.

Until the 2011 ban, hunters often took the pelt, claws, and skull of the polar bears they killed.

Global warming is caused by humans, which makes people the polar bear's biggest threat. Sea ice is the bears' **habitat**. It is where polar bears live, hunt, den, and raise their cubs. Some scientists estimate that, if the ice continues to disappear, polar bears could be extinct within 100 years. But scientists are trying to spread the word about the polar bears' problem. Polar bears are listed as threatened under the Endangered Species Act. This status means they could become endangered and even extinct.

However, helping the polar bear is an uphill battle. The Endangered Species Act only applies to the United States. And American Indians can still hunt polar bears for food. The bears are also hunted in Canada, Greenland, and parts of Russia. Some hunters believe that polar bears are not in danger. They say that the polar bear population is actually increasing. Others continue the hunt because of the money that can be earned by sport hunting.

People have been working for decades to protect the bear and its habitat. Polar bears are a part of a unique **ecosystem** that exists in, on, and under the ice. The ecosystem begins with microscopic organisms called phytoplankton, and ends with polar bears. They all depend on a healthy Arctic habitat to exist. Protecting the polar bears means also protecting many plants and animals.

The Arctic Ecosystem

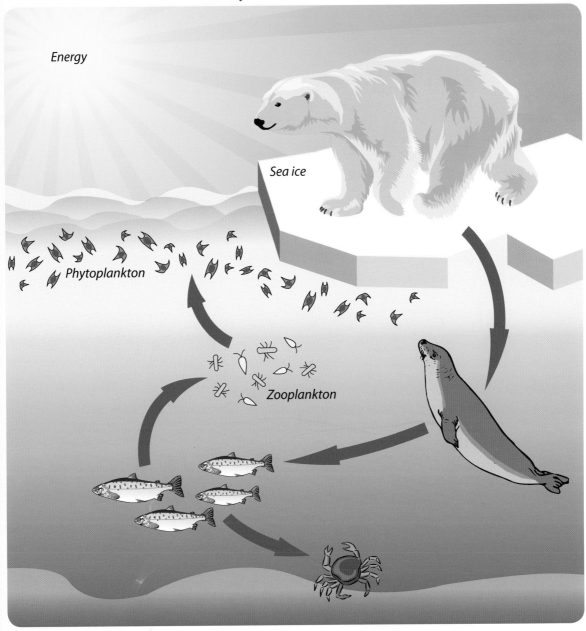

Energy

Sea ice

Phytoplankton

Zooplankton

habitat: the natural place and conditions in which a plant or animal lives

ecosystem: a system of living and nonliving things in an environment

Saving the Ice Bear

Much of the work to save polar bears is being done by kids just like you. Each year, Polar Bears International holds a contest called Project Polar Bear. Teams of 14- to 17-year-olds compete to reduce carbon dioxide (CO_2) in their community. CO_2 is a major greenhouse gas. Project Polar Bear contestants have reduced CO_2 by almost 200 million pounds! Less CO_2 gas in the **atmosphere** means less risk to polar bear habitat.

The winning team from 2010 was a group of 14-year-old girls with lightbulbs on the brain. They taught their community the benefits of compact fluorescent lightbulbs (CFLs). They gave away CFL bulbs at events and worked with local businesses to switch to CFL bulbs. The result? They reduced CO_2 by 1.5 million pounds (0.7 million kg). What a bright idea!

atmosphere: the mixture of gases that surrounds Earth

Change, One Lightbulb at a Time

What if every house in the United States replaced just one regular bulb with a CFL bulb?

- Enough energy would be saved to light 3 million homes for a year

- $600 million in energy costs would be saved every year

- Greenhouse gas emissions would be reduced by 9 billion pounds (4 billion kg) every year. That's about the same amount of emissions as produced by 800,000 cars!

One way you can help polar bears at home is doing the Charger Challenge. Get together with a few of your friends for a contest of energy saving. Pick an electronic device in your house. Televisions, cell phones, or video game players are great choices. Keep a log of how many hours the device is plugged into the wall. After a week, get together to compare numbers. The person with the lowest score wins. Afterward, teach your family that electronics use energy when they're plugged in. They use energy even if they're turned off. Show how much energy you could save by unplugging things when they're not in use!

There are other ways to be green at home. Turn the lights off at home when you leave the room. Walk, skate, or ride a bike instead of driving. Plant a tree or shrub in your yard and watch it grow. Learn how to mulch your yard, collect rainwater for plants, or start a compost pile. Sort your recyclables instead of throwing them in the trash.

It's important to talk to your friends and family about the threat of global warming. Discuss alternative energy sources and figure out what you can do to make a difference. Changes need to be made if polar bears are to survive. Encourage your family to make that change together!

There is still time to save the Great Bear. By using less energy and learning about global warming, you are the great bear's greatest hope. Small steps and big ideas can make a difference. The future of the planet, and of the polar bear, is much brighter when we all work together.

Only people can slow down or stop global warming. Without our help, the Great Bear of the north will be gone in the next century.

Glossary

atmosphere (AT-muhss-fihr)—the mixture of gases that surrounds Earth

blubber (BLUH-buhr)—a thick layer of fat under the skin of some animals; blubber keeps animals warm

calorie (KA-luh-ree)—a measurement of the amount of energy that food gives you

climate change (KLY-muht CHAYNJ)—a significant change in Earth's climate over a period of time

ecosystem (EE-koh-sis-tuhm)—a system of living and nonliving things in an environment

embryo (EM-bree-oh)—an animal that is just beginning to grow before birth or hatching

extinct (ik-STINGKT)—no longer living; an extinct animal is one that has died out with no more of its kind

floe (FLOH)—a large sheet of floating ice

global warming (GLOH-buhl WARM-ing)—rise in the average worldwide temperature of the troposphere

greenhouse gases (GREEN-houss GASSES)—gases in a planet's atmosphere that trap heat energy from the sun

habitat (HAB-uh-tat)—the natural place and conditions in which a plant or animal lives

hibernate (HYE-bur-nate)—to spend winter in a deep sleep; animals hibernate to survive low temperatures and lack of food

Read More

Hirsch, Rebecca E. *Top 50 Reasons to Care about Polar Bears: Animals in Peril*. Top 50 Reasons to Care about Endangered Animals. Berkeley Heights, N.J.: Enslow Publishers, 2010.

Olson, Gillia. *Polar Bears' Search for Ice: A Cause and Effect Investigation*. Animals on the Edge. Mankato, Minn.: Capstone Press, 2011.

Rosing, Norbert. *Polar Bears*. Richmond Hill, Ont.: Firefly Books, 2010.

Internet Sites

FactHound offers a safe, fun way to find Internet sites related to this book. All of the sites on FactHound have been researched by our staff.

Here's all you do:

Visit *www.facthound.com*

Type in this code: 9781429684323

Check out projects, games and lots more at
www.capstonekids.com

Index